Praise For Un' Spoken

"Un' Spoken's natural ability to rhythmically intertwine words in the English language is amazing, as she has mastered how to minister to hearts and souls through her artistry. She is no stranger to the microphone, but instead a vessel who has discovered her God-given purpose through the art of prose. Her poetry is that breath of fresh of air, determined to give relief to your spirit and a resounding word of encouragement to the negative attributes that once lived in you. Un' Spoken's artistry is life changing and heart-probing. Her rhythm is love which is the very attribute that characterizes her spirit as a person and as an artist."

~ Chundria Stanback -Flair TV Productions, Inc.

"Un' Spoken's words are like blood in my body it keeps flowing & pushing to keep me going forward."

~ Jermaine Robinson

"When Un' Spoken speaks she gives you her heart and soul, with a realness that's undeniable. She's a poets poet, and as an artist myself I have been and still am inspired by her. "

~ Scott Carlton

"Un' Spoken, one word - truth"

~ Kelly Fletcher

"Strong Delivery and Passion when Un' Spoken Speaks"

~Keith King

"Breathtaking and captivating. Un' Spoken leaves you like her name...Speechless."

~ Mr. Spoken Red - Spoken Red Enterprises, LLC

Breathe Deep & Think About It

A Book of Poetry

By: Un'Spoken

Get Soul Productions

Chicago Il, 60628

www.AllAboutUnSpoken.Com

Breathe Deep & Think About It

A Book Of Poetry

Un' Spoken

ISBN: 978-1-105-28991-0

Book Design by: Get Soul Productions

Photos by: Get Soul Productions , Artis Chapman & ICU LookinTv

Editing by: Jonathan W. Cassell Sr.

9 8 7 6 5 4 3 2 1

Manufactured in the United States of America

For information regarding special discounts for bulk purchases or booking,Please contact Get Soul Productions @ 1-317.572.SOUL or Booking@AllAboutUnSpoken.Com

~Dedications~

This, my first book is affectionately dedicated to:
My daugthers Koriyona and Keyontea. You both
Continue to give me a reason to want to breathe
On a daily basis. Always remember that you can
do ALL things through Christ who WILL strengthen
you.

To my Husband Jonathan who has supported me
from day one. No matter how crazy or difficult
the idea, you've, always told me to go for it. And
while I was going for it, you never left my side. I love
you today, I love you tomorrow and I'll love you
forever.

To my beautiful Mom, Shirley Holloway (yes I put
Your entire name in my book) and to my awesome
God Daddy, James Rogers for accidently giving me
so much to write about.

And, of course, to my many HATERS... Thanks for
Telling me that I couldn't do it!
Keep up the good work.

~Poetic Introduction~

…And now I understand that which those who over stand understand.

I know the secrets that have forever endured through to the end of ends

My Destiny has always lied between my unopened hands. And because I am a chosen God's people I am destine to demand VICTORY

Parts of my history was set into place on yesterday, so today I stand brand new. I'm Strong enough to feel past your walled energy, in order to see the real you.

Your true identity will show my path to be narrow, but quick. Largeenough for only you, me and God to fit.

I admit, I am not yet complete, but I declare that everything is still wonderful for me.

Un' Spoken

Table of Contents

8 - Part One: You Wonder How I Got Here...

9 - Father, Where Have You Been?
11 - Ghetto Poetry
12 - Childhood Memories
14 - I'm Home (Washington State)
16 - A Baller's Dream
18 - I Was There! (Muffled Screams)

22 - Part Two: I know it Ain't Easy...

23 - I Wanna Speak
26 - Ramble # 1
26 - Ramble #2
27 - No Peace
27 - I Wonder
30 - Get Your Life in Order
31 - That Black Man Over There
36 - No Common Sense
40 - Skeletons In Her Closet

43 - Part Three: It's Ok to Love...

44 - Last Night
45 - Ramble # 3
45 - Questions About Love
46 - Please Be Real
47 - Convenient
49 - Ramble # 4
50 - Ramble #5

51 - Part Four: Live Life and Learn From It...

52 - Ramble #6
52 - Single Parent
54 - Nigger Woman
58 - Again
60 - Superior or Not
62 - Ramble #7
63 - You Don't Know Me
66 - Can't Write

70- Part Five: Givin God His Due Praise

71 - Keep Writing
77 - The Story
80 - I Need to Talk to You
83 - Talents
85 - Help Me
86 - Grace has brought me thus far

PART ONE

You Wonder How I Got Here...

Father Where Have You Been?

I met you on AGAIN today,

For what certainly seemed like the first time.

And my feeling on this matter are still some how unclear...

I'm not Happy

I'm not Mad

I'm not Sad or Even Disgusted.

Just Shocked.

It's been 7 whole Years and You spoke to me as if the time were equal to only 7 days, one week.

But I guess your mind is the first thing to go when you're living a "shady" life!

I wonder what made you change your mind about being a father

Was it love?

Was it guilt?

Curiosity about my life and what you've missed?

Or, was it the undeniable, fact that since I'm now over the age of 18, you would no longer have to worry about the back pay of the infamous child support?

...And we talked,

we talked for what seemed like an eternity.

But for some strange reason an eternity could still not catch up with my lifetime.

And between the telephone operator and the unknown family members who just wanted to say an innocent hello, I think that I'm the only one who truly felt out of place.

And I never got the chance to ask the most important questions:

Father, where have you been?

What did you do while you were there?

What made you change your mind about being MY father?

And how long do I have to get to know you, before you start to live that "shady life' again?

Ghetto Poetry (thoughts of a Child)

Ghetto Love

Ghetto Mix

Ghetto Bills

Ghetto Fix it

Ghetto Touched

Ghetto Tears

Ghetto Knows

Ghetto Hears

Momma Always Saw

Cause Grandma Always Told

Auntie Taught me, that together we grows in the Ghetto.

YES I said grows, Cause we ain't spelling nothing right in the Ghetto.

When my feet touch concrete and dirt, I now where I am because my hood and my God come to my mind first.

& Together we know that it's all for a purpose and He had to have a plan.

So if you don't plan on lending a dollar or a hand, then don't come stand in my Ghetto.

Ghetto Fears Love

Ghetto Mixes Give

Ghetto Bills rob peter to Pay

§ for Ghetto Fixes we Pray.

My Ghetto Touch Knows, that your Ghetto Tears will Roll.

Grandma always saw before momma

§ TOGETHER we'll grow old in the Ghetto.

Childhood Memories

Picture me now: ENGLEWOOD!

Block 65

I'm only 4

Standin on the bus stop with all the big boyz.

See, we had to take the bus er' where, here and there.

In case you didn't know, the bus would take you wherever you wanted ta go as long you had you a transfer.

But Me, I got on fa free, cause I was slightly higher than yo knee.

Dez are my childhood memories.

Had ta be downtown at least by 5, cause Goldblats closed at 6. But I'm tryn ta hurry back cause Bon Bon was sick. Moms tryin ta fit me wit these ugly kicks, plus my leg startin to hurt cause I got a bruise on my knee from fightin the boyz cross the street.

Dez are my childhood memories.

Moma calling me from down the street, 1st warning... "Come Eat!" and so she could do my hair.

But I was too busy rockin to a beat from somebody's car parked way down there.

I aint wanna go see what she wanted, cause I already knew.

But I knew if I didn't make it in before them street lights flicked on... I was done! Threw!

I promise, you'd hear me screaming from the other end of the block.

I still got a scab on my arm from a few days ago when I got popped.

Dez are my childhood memories.

You've got yours and I've got mines.

I could NEVER leave my past behind.

There were so many things I learned (weather heard or unheard), things that could never be burned.

Some lessons to you may seems upsured, but they come from a street, where in the world you might not be able to stand the heat, but you could always rock your worries away to a beat.

And your boys and your girls where always there when you needed a helping hand.

They were even there when you needed a can of corn.

That's what real friends are for...

...And dez are MY childhood memories.

I'm Home! (Washington State)

Today I looked outside of my borrowed window

§ for the first time in my life I SAW peace.

I said hello to the world and from the mountains the world said hello back.

I watched the trees stand proud § I heard the birds sing out loud

§ the air was so clean § clear that I was tempted to taste the rain.

§ I remembered sadder days – for the "they's" say that if you don't know where you've been you won't know where your going. § you're more than destined to return where you started- AND I DON'T WANNA GO BACK!

I don't wanna go back to the days when pain was the majority § pleasure rarely played a part in anything.

I don't wanna go back to the days when everything surrounding my ghetto was completed by chaos, noise § Pollution.

The substitutions for what should've have been, wasn't discovered until 2400 mile later, but I found it.

Ghetto said that it didn't exist, but I found it.

Chaos and noise tired its best to distract me with its well thought out antics, but I found it.

§ pollution tried so damned hard to fog up my mentals, but I found it.

§ now its mine.

Before I left this morning, I made sure that I left my no longer borrowed windows open. For my hopes are, that my newfound peace would reek havoc on my new, No longer borrowed surrounding.

A Balla's Dream

Clean cut

White kicks

A phat ball in my pocket to jag off with.

Its on!

From the beginning of my day until the very end, this is how my balla's dream begins.

I can buy what I want.

I already got what I need.

Big silver herringbone chain and it's the 90's, so I got to rock ALL my rings.

I gotta have me a truck,

§ it's gotta have big beats and funky sounds.

Its gotta have rims, lays and tinted windows all the way around,

Cause if it don't look like a balla, act like a balla and ride like a balla, then the balla in you really ain't true.

My gear, its tight.

I always come into yo presents with all the latest fades.

Fila

Nike

& Tommy Hilfiger

On dat @%*.

Shorties gotta look up to me

5' 5 and up gotta look down.

Not really aware that jealousy gets you jacked and hating gets you clowned!

Cell phone in my pocket and the pager beeping while Im speakin.

My favorite code 3605, that means that my spot is heatin.

My crews stay watchin my back,

Keepin an eye on my loot.

Maybe its because im so got damned cute or maybe its because Im a balla.

And this is my balla theme.

So why dream?

Cause where im from things ain't always what they are or as easy as they seem.

But if I dream, in my mind I can create any scene.

And in my balla dream... I can have anything.

I was There! (Muffled Screams)

I had heard her many screams of apology.

And I had heard her 4 small children pleading and begging for their daddy to just leave their mommy ALONE!

I heard the glass shatter and fall like rain drops, from above my head.

I felt her warm, yet AIDS infested blood, touch and splatter slightly above my right knee.

I felt panic as I franticly washed it way.

I quickly surveyed my skin for an opening, there was none and I was presumed ok,

but she wasn't.

I had just witnessed her get thrown out of the window...the 13th floor window.

I watched 8 police cars, that's 16 police officers pass right by the murder scene

NOW WHAT DID SHE DO TO DESERVE THIS?

Now on any other day my block was a normal police officer in habitant, but not today…when they were NEEDED!

The frail chicken %@!* of a man know as daddy to those 4 small children, packed up, and got the hell outta town. And he took the youngest child with him, because she could not yet speak. And so he figured that she would not remember.

STUPID!

She couldn't talk,

But she could cry.

And that is exactly what she did; she continued to cry for her mommy.

I cried too, as I motionlessly watched her mother's lifeless body being tossed haphazardly into a body bag.

Her name was listed Jane Doe before the ambulance had even left the block and a few days later, I heard word that her body would be dumped in a borrowed box that was much to small for her frame, in a cemetery that was much to far to travel.

But I went anyway.

ALONE!

And alone I learned that her now 3 small children would become wards of the state.

And alone once again I cried.

I cried for families with broken homes.

I cried for mothers who have to do it all alone.

I cried for heartaches and pains.

I cried because no one even knew her name.

I just cried!

That day after visiting, when I returned home, I took the elevator up to the 13th floor and I peeked out of the already boarded up window of apartment 1308.

The chalk stains of her memory had already been washed away by the rain. And she had already been forgotten.

Her story never appeared on the local news and there was no real lessons learned from her death.

And it's been a little while now, but I still cry, but I no longer stop on the 13th floor anymore. Because the last time that I did, apartment 1308 had become occupied by a family whom had no idea of what had happened there before their arrival!

See, She has 4 small children – just like the other family.

She stays home while he goes to work – just like the other family.

And one day in passing I heard her muffled screams of apology – just like the other family.

And I refuse to listen to her 4 small children pleading or begging or crying for their daddy to just leave their mommy alone.

Part Two

I Know it Ain't Easy...

I Wanna Speak

I wanna speak about not being able to speak

Cause lately I been feeling like my soul can't think

I can't write

I can't work

I can't sleep

I can't eat

There's no mic in my life, so why live?

Why wake up in the morning just to do it all over again?

My words come from within

It seeps out from somewhere so deep that only my God can see.

Only God can see the true me.

The true me loves the stage.

No lights needed,

Just a pen and a page.

I feel trapped in a cage.

Sentenced to a life without words!

No one allowing for my story to be told.

And it's so cold in here that I can't fake it.

And I don't mean to be rude,

But forget about $20 and hour,

Forget about this meaningless power

Don't call me Miss Manager any more

Cause I no longer wanna work in your retail store

Shifting products and folding clothes

While you turn up your nose

As if you're better than me.

Free is all I really wanna be

Free to be free.

I wanna speak about how speaking liberates me.

I know what God has for me,

He gave me this gift to use it.

So if I can't use it, I might as well lose it.

I need to be heard nation wide,

While my family sits on the side lines full of pride.

While my children whispers "That's My Mommy".

While my husband stands behind me.

I have no joy without my words,

And to you this may seem a little far-fetched or absorbed,

But you don't understand,

I was sent here to do this

so without words I feel like a women with no man.

Christmas without Christ.

I feel like I'm on sale with no price.

Outta place...

Like a stranger with no face

Or a security guard with no mace

Stupid

Useless

I can't continue to do this

I have to pursue this

Cause I need to speak

Ramble #1

I cry from the inside so you can't see
Because this is not my home!!
This is not my home!!
If this were my home I would be free to
roam and do as I please and indeed I would
be pleased to do-me.
I cant be anybody else...
So except me as I come and when
I finally find my home you'll be welcome
to be yourself as well.

Ramble #2

brain clouds
rain clouds
the same clouds as yesterday
they say it's gonna be wet
so you'd better bring an umbrella

NO Peace

He keeps his eyes covered
so you can't see his pain.
She holds her head down
and her tears water the earth
like rain...drops.

My people are hurting and its like I see them choking, but I don't know CPR!
When they are in stress I feel it right in the middle of my heart.
And it tears me apart.
It so sad how we keep stabbing each other in the back.
the same ones you swear are your people will repeat your secrets right back!
damn..............
Aint no peace on the block!!

I Wonder

I wonder

If I drowned at this very instant,

Who would save my life first?

Him or her?

Or perhaps the one who isn't even near?

I wonder

If I died right now this very instant

Who would hurt the most?

Mom, Dad or those who never knew that I existed?

I wonder

if I cry, who would dry my face?

And who is it that really holds my fate in the palm of their hands

Who would hand me a towel to wipe away the sand if I fall?

I wonder who even cares at all.

And sometimes I wonder,

If anybody understands me

I think I found him, but I wonder

How long he'll stay.

And as we lay, is he thinking about leaving?

I wonder

what it is that keeps me breathing?

And why is it that when I pay attention to life

Breath gets shorter?

And I wonder

Will I have a son or daughter?

I wonder

What makes me love myself

And why is it harder for someone else

... to love me ?

I wonder

how long I'll stay alive?

And I wonder

If it'll get harder by year or Day to just survive?

I wonder

why I don't know?

And if I go this way

I wonder, which other way I'll go?

I wonder how long I'll stay?

And until that day- when my questions are answered

My wonder remains.

Get Your Life in Order

For the life of me I can't begin to understand my people.

We have become so dark and so see through...transparent.

And it's apparent that the roads that we have chosen to travel have no end.

We've become dead!

Dead like incinerated dollar bills.

Dead like broken Homes that produce

broken babies.

Killed!

Life less and unburied.

Walking tombs!

Only having our selves to lose.

Battle bruised!

See, I am a product of my environment,

but I left the hood once they stopped hiring.

Broke!

Desperate and uneducated...

And just like you they had already anticipated my failure.

But I refused to give up

Battered and weak, I shook my own wings and I lifted them up.

And when I became a woman I put away

Childish things as in stuff and people that I didn't need.

So, See Me now!!

Come fly with me

Let me take you on a journey

So we can both see how things should be.

That Black Man over There

See that man bending and creeping in the corner?

Yeah that black man over there.

Once upon a time

He was a boy

Sitting in the same spot

Playing with the same toy.

His momma sold her body

And his daddy sold crack.

So his whole life he promised he would never travel back to the place where he grew up

Because it was such a hellish pitiful sight.

So all night long

He rocks

And turns

And fights

In that corner

That black man over there in the corner.

He grew up on a street where everyone stood for their own.

And seven out of ten of his homeboys were out there all alone.

With No one to talk to,

No one to trust

All they knew was that the street life was a must, and If you wanted to survive

Or better yet just fit in...

you had to fen

Or at least pretend

That you were hard,

And could make it on your own

While on the back of your mind you played that

Nobody loves me song.

Everybody went through the same thing,

But the next man never really knew

Caused he was stressed out on his own

And wasn't too much worried about you.

So now that same man is hiding

Doing just what he said he wouldn't do.

Shooting up with dope

Cause he thought it would help him cope

And relieve his mind

And still he's in that same corner

Hiding from the world,

With three pairs of pants

And a long tan trench coat

Smelling like piss and alcohol

With white stains around his nose

From snorting up all that dope.

Yes! that black man over there!

He could have been somebody

He could have done something with his life

But instead he just took that bland knife

And cut up his arms just missing his veins

Cause he was mad that his own momma, due to her own addictions, didn't even know his name

Or care.

If somebody would have just told him that

There was a God up there

And if somebody would have been there

Instead of peeking through the curtains

Everyday wondering what to say

That corner would be empty

And his promises would be full filled, and in times revealed

That man

Bending and creeping

In that corner...

Yes that black man over there,

Would have been reaching

And preaching

With the many black men who made it out, to tell their stories.

Yes that black man over there

No Common Sense

I cry for you,

Not because I feel sorry for you

Or because I feel pity for your situation,

But because I knew you could do better.

I watched you

And I saw you as you grew up with the same opportunities that I had.

I sat with you in classroom 400 of the neighborhood public school

The first time, the second time, the third time and even the fourth time you got suspended,

But then the fifth time came and I guess you just didn't care anymore.

I was there many times when your mother had questions as to why you seemed to be there at home with her, more than at school where you should have been

I heard your response

Change from the familiar, "I Don't Know"

To the newly invented "Them teacher just don't like me"

And that's where it ended.

Everything came to a screeching halt here.

The excuses,

The respect,

The hiding,

the shoe boxes full of money and marijuana.

The fear of getting caught,

Education,

even your common sense ceased to exist after This Day.

You walked in on your mother praying for you one day and had a fit

Simply Not wanting any help, because according to yo' literature yo' boys had your back,

But that turned out to be temporary.

Because soon, you started making too much money.

You came up a little too fast.

And when you thought your boys were the

One's that put you on,

Till this das, they still want you dead.

Most of them have already met their own graves.

So now you find yourself by yourself once again, but only by choice.

Your not doing good, but you could be doing worse

You're minus friends, but you don't have any known enemies.

You sleep from place to place every night, but at least you sleep.

You're minus money, but at least you had some in the first place. (you reminisce on those days frequently)

You going day by day just existing, but you're still here.

How this happened, nobody but God knows

Hummmm....

9th grade education

Aids

3 STD's, lonely,

No sisters, brothers,

No mother, (she had a beautiful funeral that you weren't even a part of)

You weren't even in the house to save her

And that's to bad cause she could have lived,

But she gave up fighting after she realized, you had left months before and no one would be coming home anytime soon.

She gave up, - maybe that's where you got that from.

Nah, I doubt it- cause she didn't teach you that much anyhow.

And the mothers of those 6 children

That you helped to produce won't teach then much either.

Damn!

What happened?

I watched,

I saw,

I heard,

I was there...

I got out, I guess I was one of the lucky one's.

I drove past our old high school today and I saw a little boy who looked just like you did when you were that age.

Class wasn't out yet, but he was.

And I cried for him, not because I felt sorry for him, or because I felt pity for his situation.

But, because somehow I knew he could do so much better.

Oh and by the way I prayed today for the first time in my whole life.

I prayed that, that young man would never loose common sense and that you would somehow someday find yours.

Skeletons in Her Closet

She has skeletons in her closet and every time she opens the door, they come screaming out and making her look like a horrible person.

I met a girl today and on the outside she was loosed and running wild, but on the inside she was hurt and I found out that on the inside she possess the heart of a lost child.

She has skeletons in her closet

and every time she opens the door they come screaming out.

Her clothes were tight and revealing and her face was over made up and under development. You could tell she was just a kid.
And i heard some old lady mumble "what a shame"
as she walked by.
But what's a shame?
The fact that she wakes up everyday, gets ready and goes about the same routine.
turns the same tricks she turned the day before. then goes home to get some sleep and do it all over again
tomorrow?
Or is it you? You who just looks?
You who mock her, without even knowing her
Troubles or her back story?
You who has become her main source of income, her number one customer?
You who show up every Tuesday at 5:00 leave by seven to get home and spend time with your family, your wife, your kids and the dog?
you!
Or you?
You pass by her every Sunday morning on your way to church, but not once have you lifted her up in prayer?
Or you who jokes " somebody need to give
her a whoopin"!!

But did you know her mama was never there!
Did you know that when she as 10 her house was raided so she hid and they couldn't find her and when she came out from the secret place everybody was dead and her heart was so hurt she cried for a little while but then
realized that wouldn't bring them back.
She figured out real quick that to get money you need a job, but she was just too young for that.
A "family friend" came along and helped her out. He put her on a stroll, showed her where to go. So from the age of 10 years old you must know that being a hoe is all she knows.

It has paid her bills and put clothes on her back
and anything else she needs her "family friend",
pimps her out to help with that.
So who's the shame you or her?
Nobody has ever stopped to give her an alternate plan.
So how is she supposed to know how is she supposed to grow
if she only knows one way?
She has skeletons in her closet and every time
she opens the door they come screaming out.
So instead of making her the shame, help her and give her
skeletons a reason to be quiet about

Part Three

It's Ok to Love...

Last Night

I was home alone last night

When I felt something touch me.

At first I thought I had ghosts,

But then I realized that they had left me a long time ago.

So I left it alone.

And it touched me again.

It touched me from my head, to my toes.

And when I screamed, " leave me alone"

It hollered back "No.... I will never go".

It sat with me on the couch,

And kept me company as I waited

And every time I told a joke

I laughed and it hated.

I went to sleep and there it was

Right next to me.

And I usually I like to sleep alone,

But last night it felt like ecstasy.

When I woke up the next morning

I was confused and I didn't know what to do.

And that's when I realized that it was you.

My mind has been boggled for far too long.

But now I can kiss confusion away.

I am free and clear all of my misery and now I can see what's really for me.

Ramble #3

I need my own him.

A him, just for me...

A him, where his scar and my rib meet.

Questions about Love

Is love supposed to become harder as it gets older?

Is that the part that makes it stronger?

Does fussing and fighting bring relationship closer?

Or is that what makes a nigga scream, "I can't stand her"?

"I love you" but do I have to like you every minute of my day?

Should I go alone anyway when I'm not in the mood and I don't want to play?

Who's to say who's given the answers?

Who knows what to do?

Well you tell him that I said this:

"This Being in love stuff is given me the blues"

Yea I am complaining but I ain't going away

I just got a few questions about love.

Like how do you get it to stay?

Please be real

Please be real,

Because the feelings that you make me feel are real.

The smile that escaped from my soul when you are near are real.

My children loved you before me,

And I wanna take that as a sign for me...

to love you too.

But I need to know that the you that you show me,

is the you that you really are.

And the spirit that you have sent after my heart

Will constantly be around.

So please for God's sake, be real.

Convenient

I see it in your eyes,

But I can't determine if its truth.

Can't trust my heart no more cause it keeps leaving me lonely.

Long story, so we won't discuss that!

I can't look at you without smiling, but that don't seem to mean much.

I can feel your chemistry without even being touched

So I mask my emotions, or should I say that I make them go away.

I really just wanna lay on your chest

And breathe and sleep, more like rest and think about things that shouldn't worry me.

Cause you seem safe.

Dark

Tall

Faithful

Creative

And handsome

You are my list

And I felt you release your spirit into me

The first time we kissed

But I'm scared so I'd rather hold on to

something that doesn't, and never will exist...

It's convenient.

Ramble #4

I see cracks of sunlight through my door

And people are already walking around and awake in my dreams...

How did they get here before me?

And where am I anyway?

There's no address on the buildings in front of me!

I guess I just got here by Faith...

I need to write about this, before it drives me insane.

I'm dreaming of awards and the BET stage.

But I keep waking up in the same place... Still alone, even he's gone.

- And where is his face Anyway?
- Why won't you let me see him?

I need some progress.... Is all my work in vain?

Why can't I stop my inner me from this eternal pain

Who should I trust? Which path should I walk?

Ramble #5

She sees him in the privacy of her own serenity.

She closes her eyes and he is still there

She opens them and there he still remains.

He is stationary because he is HER man and she is his woman...

...And there...

Forever...

They will remain.

Part Four

Live Life and Learn From It...

Ramble #6

When tomorrow might not come, your best bet is to live harder on today & PRAY somehow becomes the word that makes it to everyone's lips.

When you may not see the next minute you'll always have something else to do.

And no matter what time it is, it'll never be enough time.

There's always more stuff...

The only advice I can give is to live every second like an emergency evacuation...

CAREFULLY and with great precision...

Single Parent

Beaten

Broken

Drained

But PROUD

No body was there to help with the bills,

So we just went without.

Couldn't afford a whole living room set, but we had a house.

Not enough food, but we made it stretch and better yet ends always met.

Tired

Sick

Depressed

But Still here!

It was dark on my street, but momma said "don't fear"...

And she wasn't just talking about the streets, but life.

She taught us so much right...

Alone...

We Growed with just momma.

Hollered and cursed, But she loved us.

Hugged us.

Alone...

We growed with just momma.

She was a woman of many others.

She was black

She was White

Hispanic and Asian

Short

Tall

Slim

And Wide...

She comes in all different kinds

My Momma was a Single Parent and she's made me Proud

Nigger Woman

Dark

Closed

Disposed

Empty

& suspended.

Though your eyes this is how you see me.

The "nigger"

You see me and think that I'm committed to this state of life.

You see me living messes up and fighting my own kind.

You see me scared of my own self.

My tone has too much melatonin for you.

Too much nigger...

And you think, that my heart is dead, but this contemplation rest only inside of your own heads.

Your bad experience made you mad, while me it made stronger and pride convinced some of us to sing old spirituals.

We made most words up because we didn't know the real ones.

I wasn't there and neither were you, but I hear that more than a few of my mothers were Queens.

Fathers... All Kings and my brother laid his palms on the sandstone bricks of the Egyptian pyramids.

So tell me, how did I become your nigger?

How did I become your nigger woman?

How did I become another woman on your plantation full of niggers?

And here you still stand with your tired 7-minute speech predicting to control my life for the next 400 years.

But now here I am in 2012 and I've done the math and chalked it up to the numerical equation that displays the fact that is only year 292 and that leaves you 138 years to go.

And I stand strong because I know that you've already messed up.

You messed up when you "let" me vote

You messed up when you "let" me choose my own seat on the bus...

You "let" me join your army and a nigger with a M16 Riffle can't be considered a punk.

(uncle sam's already got one bullet hole in his ass, so I don't understand why you keep turning your back on me.)

As if you trust me...

When according to you, I'm not even supposed to trust myself.

You tried to condition me to envy what you had, tried to make me think that was best for me.

I guess you comparing me to a horse helped to put you at ease.

And you really thought that supplying my needs while beating my soul mate and me would bring us to our knees.

...and it did, but only due to my pain

Yes, rain makes mud.

But, shedding blood don't make me love...

Especially when you shed not..

When you cry not...

When you feel where I come from, not.

Know this: IAM NOT YOUR NIGGER ANYMORE!

I am the woman you wish your women could be.

I am the woman you wish your men could still freely see.

I am the mother you wish your children still had.

I am not your slave anymore and I know that makes you so sad, but I don't care because I've been pissed off for long enough.

BUT…I continued to grow

I got over it

Now I am grown and my ancestors are long gone.

I didn't pick no cotton and I don't maintain the back of a slave.

And your name has never been Masta' to me.

I have been free from the beginning and will continue to be for an eternity.

So while you sit faithfully in your afro American history class trying to learn me, take this one note: IAM NOT YOUR NIGGER.

Again

Again

I am Here,

the one place where I hate to be.

The street between if and then

No and why not

Go and stop.

I stand here contemplating tomorrows,

borrowing answers that sound good enough to just to get by.

But I don't know where I'm going once I get "there".

I'm not even sure where "there" is

I'm not even sure where the care is.

I'm not sure of anything right now!

How can I go on without letting myself get lost in the struggle?

How can I go on without letting my past recreate my future?

Again.

These things happen in life.

But you can't let it define you...

I can't let it define me...

Please UNDERSTAND me.

I need to be understood.

The way I move, the reason I breathe defines me...

I just want peace...

AGAIN.

Superior or Not

Do you think that you are superior to me because you live in Beverly Hills?

And because your house is bigger than mine?

Do you feel you are superior to me because you shop at expensive stores?

(which don't necessarily mean that you are actually spending money)

...And because your school tuition is higher than mine

That you are superior to me?

Well, you must be outta your mind!!

Because the color of your skin and your zip code

Don't mean a damn thing to me.

The prices you pay,

The type of clothes you wear,

and the thickness of yo mamas wallet...

Don't faze me at all.

That visa card you got for your birthday.

And those Versace Dresses you wasted money on yesterday.

Mean absolutely nothing!

(And I do mean nothing)

At all...

Cause this is my call...

I'm rich in love,

Not dimes or dollars.

My dad wears a blue collar, because White gets dirty to quick!

Even quicker when you're busy stealing from the poor to give to the rich.

And your whole out look makes me sick!

See, I got name brand clothes too!

And everybody knows,

That just like you I live in a house with four walls, so you ain't done nothing fancy at all.

You're not superior ...

But inferior

Because of your state of mind.

And you have now officially begun to waste my time.

So do you still think that you are superior to me?

Ramble #7

Illusions precede me.

So you don't see me coming

But I got this feeling that even if I were in plain sight.

I would still, to you, be invisible.

Invisible as hell...

When I walk past you- you only feel the air.

And because your visions fell you, I feel your fears...

You Don't Know Me

You don't even know me, and I wish that I could explain myself in depth.

Because my life has been filled with a lot of tears and crying.

A lot of pain

A lot of stress and a whole lot of test.

But not just regular test,

Test for those who've been chosen.

The kind when the devil is constantly provoking you?

And God keeps seeing you through.

And you keep wondering who's been holding you.

And that's when you open your eyes and realize that God has chosen YOU..

I've Been Chosen...

Cause If I had my choice I'd use my Voice for anything, but this.

So It's obvious that I've been destine for this.

From the time that I picked up a Pen and started to write.

When I was the smallest and the youngest of the crowd and I always had to fight, just to keep my bike.

When I went through things that I would not even wish on my enemies.

When I screamed at the top of my lungs and it still seemed as if nobody was hearing me.

God was preparing me for this.

So I sit here in the midst of my troubles and I begin to understand who I am.

So, you don't even Know me!

I understand that my chest is full of adverbs and nouns and... I now have words pushing outta my mouth, and they keep forcing me to write them down.

I've got harmony in my kiss and poetry in my kiss... and Un' Spoken's got so much to say, that when you leave my presence, your mind will mimic me and your soul will remember me.

I dream word plays, so that's means that my words don't play.

And I could care less if you choose to not listen, because I've learned to continue to spit anyway.

Because YOU don't know me!

And while I've been trying to explain Myself in depth, I'm on the verge of giving up, because most of the worlds not ready yet.

I keep randomly screaming "FUCK IT! You Don't UNDERSTAND!... We hold the power of these prophetic words, songs and phrases in our hands". We've been destine for this... so to us this is seriousness.

But some of ya'll be taking it too light...

(I'm Hungry and I'm really thirsty) But I choose not to feed until I get life right.

So if you never remember my name...

Just remember that my claim is that I'm chosen (sent by God).

And remember that I love a crowd that agrees and let's they heads nod! The nod fuels the fire, so with the right crowd you can feel like, that's all you need and you can't get no higher.

And All I desire, is for the earth to know who I am.

This is why I do the best that I possibly can.

This is way I stay up and sweat tears in the middle of the night.

I don't do this for Man..

I don't do this simply to prove that I can.

I'm not trying to gain respect from you.

I only need you to know.. That THIS IS WHAT I DO!

Can't Write

Can't write about shit now a days

My mind stays stuck like there's bricks in the way

This world is giving me foreplay

But I cant cum, cause the ones I love aint giving me none.

No fun and no pleasure, just hard work and sweat.

And I keep seeing these visions in my head, but I ain't got to em yet.

I'm taking bets and I'm losing.

They've got a fork in the road so I'm caught choosin.

And I look at my reflection in the mirrors of my tear drops and I ask myself: Who do you think you are fooling?

No help?

Still stressed!

So I keep it moving.

I JUST NEED TO SCREAM! ...to let off some steam.

I need to scream in order to release some of these things from me.

I came to realize that I was special when I was a youngin/a shorty... When we rapped about bottles of Moet, but we could only afford 40's.

I've been carrying this weight on my shoulders that never gets lighter and I've never gotten any real respect, because I'm only considered to be a lower class writer.

I'm only self-published and I've never been signed, but my enemies have found a way to steal my name, and my rhymes!

But all the time I stay smiling

The old me woulda smoked one to em and kept grinding and never-minding the fact that, that shit really hurts.

Not trying to go back to my old ways, because I've done more then enough dirt.

I've kicked up enough dust, and although I'm civilianized now, I STILL will SNAP! So please don't test me, just trust that I try not to clown, because I've already knocked enough of my blessing down dealing with other folks.

I don't fight no more!

I just write poetry and tell real stupid jokes!

Im on a mission to not allow that bad angel to provoke thoughts within me of giving up.

Can't write about shit now a days

My mind stays stuck like there's bricks in the way

This world is giving me foreplay

But I cant cum, cause the ones I love ain't giving me none.

No appreciations and no dedication, and if I let it get into my system I would end up on medication!

This is ridiculous, and I'm tried of not being able to express my mind.

I'm tried of photo-copied Negros claiming to be one of a kind.

I'm tired of people who understand me before I even open my mouth...Just shut up listen! I doubt if you really know what I'm talking about.

Fools walking around useless. They take the time to gain all the knowledge of this world, but still prove to be clueless. They claim old school...but I know they new to this!

And that "poetry voice" is so played out. Please when you get invited to use the mic, annunciate [open your mouth real wide] so we all can know what you're talking about.

And when you get to the set, let's talk about stuff that's relevant. Nobody cares that you been freaking her man,

or that your girl gave head to your best friend... [you

knew she was a whore when you met her]... you didn't give a dame. So why should I?

I stayed high back in the day. Just to relieve these pains. Just to post pone this rain... I use to let the weed seep deep into my brain and kill my remembering cells along the way... FOOLISH!

Can't write about shit now a days

My mind stays stuck like there's bricks in the way

This world is giving me foreplay

But I cant cum, cause the ones I love ain't giving me none.

Part Five:

Giving God His Due Praise

Keep Writing

See,

I praise from my soul so until the cross

Stops bleeding can't nobody tell me That I'm wrong.

Because I know what the Lord has done for me.

And I know that I may be getting a little bit too happy too early,

But you got to understand, That I'm free.

I was in a real bad state of mind.

And if God hadn't snatched me up,

I would still be beat down and doing real hard times.

But he saw something in me

That I didn't know that I had

So I keep writing.

And it's so sad that it took this long,

For me to recover from my stupidity.

You can look down and turn nose up,

But I know there's at least one person in here that's feeling me.

I had to recognized the sin in me so that he could deliver me...

and I am so pressed for God that I got these so called saints trying to get rid of me.

But I can not continue to stand back and keep my mouth closed,

Cause God has blessed me to spit these adverbs and nouns

And I refuse to be found slipping or standing

On the side lines watchin these church folks trippin.

But don't get it twisted cause there ain't no more fighting for me.

I throw blows with pen, paper, and ink!

I have been given the power to speak!

So I will keep writing!

And giving God his due praise!

Keeping in mind that

That same somebody still needs to be saved.

Cause when he/she leaves here he's going right back to the block...

Straight back to selling rocks...

Back to the same corner where he always almost gets shot!

Just trying to eat...

Just trying to keep shoes on her baby girl's feet...

So she'll stay with him and continue to get beat...

And I know it to be true, cause one of these fools used to be me!

But God gave me the victory!

So I Keep Writing!

My dark has been real dark.

And my wrongs have been real wrong.

But some how I keep coming out Free with brand new songs.

Wait!

Hold on!

You don't get it...

My life has been hard,

But being in Christ is even harder,

Cause I've learned,

That it's up to us to carry the church

And not continue to keep it inside of the bricks

And the mortor.

And the corners ain't always infected!

And if you church folks would get up off ya knees and asses!

It could be resurrected!

It's up to us to readjust it,...

I'm so disgusted!

My souls is busted!

My key to the city has been rusted!

Because nobody wants to let truth in!

We've created a city of sin and we keep doing it

Over and over and over again!

But I keep writing.

Cause it's the only thing that keeps me sane.

And farther more, its deeply, embedded in my brain.

And it's a damn shame that this is the only way I know to relieve my pain.

I keep writing cause words somehow seem to slow down the rain.

So keep writing if you've really got something to say…

Keep writing if your only still here by God's grace…

And please don't hide behind the words…

Show us your face cause cowards seem to slow down the pace.

Keep writing if you understand this piece…

Keep writing if something on the inside of you needs to be released…

Keep writing cause somebody needs to hear…

The truth… Somebody needs to get near it.

Keep writing if God told you too!

Cause it says in his word that your talents will make room for you.

Alright,

Im gone do one more verse

Cause I see in ya eyes that sum of y'all are tired of hearing me talk about the church!

But guess what's worst?

I really don't care what you think

Cause you don't have A heaven Or A hell to put me in!

And I been done gave up on friends!

Where were you when the lights didn't work?

Where were you when I got hit by that car and I wasn't even hurt?..

And when I was getting finger fucked by the block!

Pushing weight and making drops!

Who was it that kept me outta jail?

Who was it that snatched me up outta the pits of hell?

IT WASN'T YOU!!!!

So get used to me talking about God,

Cause that's what I do,

And if you don't like it

Close ya ears Boo

I don't spit for you

And if you wasn't in the room,

Me and the mic and some empty chairs,

Would still get with it my dude

Cause my life is a miracle...So I keep Writing.

The Story

I wasn't there,

But, I do know the story...

Its a story of tears and a God of glory.

Because of what he did

We don't have to worry...

Now listen to what momma told me:

Jesus knew his purpose before it was proposed

He was placed on this earth to do only what God choose.

He was scorn,

He was talked about,

He was abused and neglected.

But in my heart, momma said

He was respected... loved...

The king of kings,

Jehovah,

Lord over all things

Messiah.

I don't want NO rocks crying out for me!

I can praise him by myself-Jesus died for ME!

Judas- got paid for the plot first,

Peter lied second.

Judas hung himself,

Pilate was confused,

Then they crucified my Lord, Took

His robe, his respect and his shoes.

Didn't you hear the news?

This is your Jesus the king of the Jews!!

Work a miracle now- take yourself down!!

You're royalty right? Wear this crown!

You thirsty? Drink this vinegar!

And we shall see in the morning if your

Disciples still remember ya!!

They mocked him- but they didn't

Know

Cause when he let the Holy Ghost go!!

The curtain from the temple was

Torn from bottom to top!

The Earth shook – The sun dropped!

The rocks split- Darkness came!

Somebody shouted - if only I would have believed in his name!

And just like it was planned still thinking with the mind of man.

They put him in a borrowed tomb...

Two guards scared- frozen like dead...

Three angels rolled back the stone...

Then Mary's came long- but was he already gone.

Jesus said – Meet me in Galilee- I am going home

And on top of the mountain Jesus, who was baptized in the name of God

Said "keep my commandments and keep me in your heart".

"I'll be back, but no one knows when, the Day- nor the hour. Not even the angels in heaven, Nor the Son, only the Father".

Momma said: Until then I am supposed to tell the story...

The Story of tears and a story of God's undying glory...

I Need to Talk to you

Jesus,

I need to talk to you.

Causes there are some things that I need you to help me do.

This year is about to end and new found commitment is striving to begin

And I need strength.

I need strength to endure so I can wade in your will.

I long for my relationship with you to be real.

Search me Lord and clean up my insides.

Continue to keep me in my right mind

Cause this world is not my own,

But I am here Lord,

So make me strong.

Help me to hold on,

And Forgive my sins,

Teach me your will so my life in you can begin...

Lord it's been a long year and I know I didn't do it on my own,

Cause if my life was in my own hands

I would be gone.

I'd be dead or missing my mind.

But you God kept me safe for 365 days and for that alone lord I say thanks.

I am grateful and you are worthy of my praise.

And if the masses decide not to get up and praise, I'll do my own thang.

we as a church really have alot to be grateful for some people wont see 2014

so lord,

I pray for your people cause with out you we won't make it another step.

Allow us not to regret anything we've done this year and move on.

give us vision, allow us to commit.

grow your will within us and make us strong.

bless your servants and give us a heart to serve.

and thank you for not giving us what we deserved.

thank you for being there when were alone.

thank you for mercy

thank you for your grace

thank you for everyone in this place.

as we strive to survive and press on in our faith bless our hearts clean us up and wipe off our slates

amen

TALENTS

I asked the lord to tell me what to say

I waited for a while and then I decided to pray

when I got off my knees with my heart ready and my soul free and clean

God said the words I would have you to say are these.

" to each of you my children I have given gifts. Some of you are castors (that means you can fish)

some of you aremenders.

some of you can sing

some of you are dancers

some of you can cook

some of you have been called to understand and interpret my book.

some of you are bench warmer and some of you are givers

someone maybe be able to remember something that

you cant remember

you can jump high and

she's better off staying low.

he may love to stay and she may

be called to go"

I say this to say that every one can do something and in the house of God everything is important even if you think its nothing.

God's main mission is to spread the gospel all over the land.

so if we have to sing it at mount zion, but you can't walk, then whose going to drive the van?

the body of christ can't move unless we all move together.

so please bow your heads with me and let me pray again.

lord, give your people the strength to allow your work to begin.

show us our talents and make us all friends because the stronger our bond the harder it is for the enemy to come in.

teach us to protect your home as if it were our own.

brick to brick

stone to stone

let us know how important we are in your heavenly plan, but also allow us to know that if one of decides not to serve you your plan will never end...amen

HELP ME

Confusion! Now that's the worst state of mind to be in.

Sittin and waitin around for my insanity to kick in!

I mean, look at this world that I live in!

a ses pool of pain, a mud puddle full of dry rain.

I wipe my face and I am still dirty, so I now look to the Lord

to make me holy.

Our lives are tainted by sin and we can never find peace

until search ourselves from within.

So to begin I pray for the love of my neighbors and eternal
love from my savior.

Lord please help my behavior cause its gettin out of hand.

The things I want in life I can't demand and my plans

never seem to fall through.

Lord please teach me how to only praise you.

if you could fix it, everything would be alright and we

could be into Round 31 of this inner fight.

Somebodies winning and its not me!

So I'm screaming! LORD Help me!

GRACE HAS BROUGHT ME THUS FAR

Came into this world- no friends just me and Jesus and I plan to leave the same way!

I understood a long time ago that I walked by faith into my grace.

And I am nowhere near being a loser.

As a matter of a fact, I am that much closer to a win.

So, while you only see this as an end for me

I'm standing here screaming, " let the games begin!"

Every now and again I sit back and contemplate my life as it use to be,

I remember when, every hurtful thing you said had the power to take hold of me.

I would sit in the dark...

Disgusted and crying alone, tryin to convince myself of my own self worth.

Whispering into the shadows just to hold on.

Too busy asking God why he made me suffer so.

To stubborn to realize that all I had to do was let go and let God!

It wasn't mine anyway.

I can't believe I wasted all those years trying to go head up with the enemy.

I wasn't prepared...

I was lost and afraid...and the devil smelled me coming miles and miles away!

See my breastplate was never tight...

And my shield was way to heavy...

I was an easy target so you know he was coming at me!

And I left the door wide open...

I made him dinner...

And I let him sit on my couch...

Had demons running through my head and all through my house...

We talking fornication and drugs, worshiping him, cause I thought I was in love- false ideas.

Used my tithes to flip a brick!

lied and told my jobs that I couldn't come to work because I was sick.

I skipped church to party, and while you were drinking

juice and eatin crackers...

I was double shotin grey goose and Bacardi, dropped my kids of with mama and disappear for days and only the lord knows the things that I did to make sure that I stayed paid.

I was a mess!

All because I didn't stop to think.

" If the lord made us in his image" then how great does that make me?

Live Life on Purpose!

CASTORS AND MENDERS

The bible says that if any man be in Christ then he is a new creature.

I am that creature!

Lord I thank you for your preachers.

I thank you for your teachers,

Because they made me see,

that I am your speaker.

So with my pen in hand I will write and tell any man who will listen.

I am called to be a Christian, because I am in Christ and because of that, God is the head of my house and my life.

Abandonments and strife is not beyond me,

because I will suffer with the toils of this earth until you sets me free.

And when I am free I will be free indeed.

And in the mean time God will provide all of my needs.

You see because I have to be a castor...

... so that my pastor can preach the word of the lord.

www.ingramcontent.com/pod-product-compliance
Lightning Source LLC
LaVergne TN
LVHW010940110826
845149LV00013B/2686

* 9 7 8 1 1 0 5 2 8 9 9 1 0 *